Contents

Life in the ocean

An octopus crawls along the ocean floor. Eight long arms look for food and places to hide. Each of its arms can stretch 9 metres (30 feet)!

Octopuses live in oceans around the world. Most octopuses like warm water. They can live in deep or shallow water.

Up close

There are more than 300 types of octopus. The smallest is less than 2.5 centimetres (1 inch) long. The biggest is 5.5 metres (18 ft) long!

An octopus has a large head.

Its head holds a brain,

a stomach and three hearts.

Octopuses have no bones. They

can squeeze into tiny spaces.

Finding food

Octopus arms are lined with many suckers. Suckers can taste what they touch. The arms reach into holes to find food.

With their long arms, octopuses snatch prey. Their sharp beaks and strong tongues can break hard shells. Octopuses eat crabs, lobsters, shrimp and fish.

Staying safe

When threatened, an octopus squirts a cloud of ink into the water. The ink confuses the predator. Then the octopus swims away.

Octopuses can camouflage themselves. That means they change colour to blend in with their surroundings. Predators find it hard to see them!

Life cycle

A female octopus lays up to 400,000 eggs. Most baby octopuses hatch in four to six weeks. An octopus lives for about one to two years.

Glossary

beak   horny projecting jaw of animals; an octopus beak looks like a parrot's beak

camouflage   pattern or colour on an animal's skin that helps it to blend in with things around it

hatch   break out of an egg

predator   animal that hunts other animals for food

prey   animal hunted by another animal for food

shallow   not deep

snatch   grab

sucker   soft, flexible part on an animal's body that is used to cling on to something

surroundings   things around something or someone

threatened   put in danger

Read more

First Encyclopedia of Seas and Oceans, Ben Denne (Usborne Publishing, 2011)

Living and Non-Living in the Ocean (Is it Living or Non-Living?) Rebecca Rissman (Raintree, 2014)

Ocean Food Chains (Food Chains and Webs), Angela Royston (Raintree, 2014)

Websites

www.bbc.co.uk/nature/life/Octopus
Discover more about octopuses.

www.dkfindout.com/uk/animals-and-nature/invertebrates/octopuses/
Learn more about octopuses and take a look at a common octopus up close!

Index